Anonymous

The Great Assises Holden in Parnassus by Apollo and His

Assessovrs

Anonymous

The Great Assises Holden in Parnassus by Apollo and His Assessovrs

ISBN/EAN: 9783337402624

Printed in Europe, USA, Canada, Australia, Japan

Cover: Foto ©ninafisch / pixelio.de

More available books at **www.hansebooks.com**

THE
GREAT ASSISES
Holden in *PARNASSUS*
BY
APOLLO
AND
HIS ASSESSOVRS:

At which Seffions are Arraigned

Mercurius Britanicus.	*The writer of Occurrences.*
Mercurius Aulicus.	*The writer of Paffages.*
Mercurius Civicus.	*The Poft.*
The Scout.	*The Spye.*
The writer of Diurnalls.	*The writer of weekly Accounts.*
The Intelligencer.	*The Scottifh Dove, &c.*

LONDON,
Printed by *Richard Cotes,* for *Edward Husbands,* and are to
be fold at his Shop in the *Middle Temple,* 1 6 4 5 .

APOLLO.

The Lord VERVLAN, Chancellor of *Parnassus*.
Sir PHILIP SIDNEY, High Constable of *Par.*
WILLIAM BVDEVS, High Treasurer.
JOHN PICVS, *Earle* of Mirandula, *High* Chamberlaine.
JVLIVS CESAR SCALIGER

ERASMUS ROTERODAM.
JUSTUS LIPSIUS
JOHN BARCKLAY
JOHN BODINE
ADRIAN TVRNEBVS
ISAAC CASAVBON
JOHN SELDEN
HVGO GROTIVS
DANIEL HEINSIVS
CONRADVS VOSSIVS
AUGUSTINE MASCARDVS

The Furours.

George Wither
Thomas Cary
Thomas May
William Davenant
Josuah Sylvester
Georges Sandes
Michael Drayton
Francis Beaumont
John Fletcher
Thomas Haywood
William Shakespeere
Philip Massinger.

The Malefactours.

Mercurius Britanicus
Mercurias Aulicus
Mercurius Civicus
The Scout
The writer of Diurnals
The Intelligencer
The writer of Occurrences
The writer of Passages
The Poste
The Spye
The writer of weekely Accounts
The Scottish Dove, &c.

A 2

Jo-

JOSEPH SCALIGER, the Cenſour of manners in *Parnaſſus.*

BEN. JOHNSON, Keeper of the Trophonian Denne.

JOHN TAYLOVR, Cryer of the Court.

EDMVND SPENCER, Clerk of the Aſſiſes.

TH E

4

The PROEME.

Uſt teares commix'd with ſtreams of guiltleſs blood
May ſhew our woes, but not their period;
For this Heaven onely can affixe: Why then,
Truſt wee to armes or ſtratagems of men?
Expecting peace, or any faire accord,
From Counſels wiſe, or the victorious Sword;
Since Heaven alone theſe evils can conclude,
Which Sinne firſt caus'd and on us did obtrude.
Could wee eject this cauſe, wee might find Peace:
For cauſes failing, then effects ſurceaſe.
Wee need demand no counſell from the Starres,
To know the iſsue of theſe bloody Warres:
No Sibylles bookes or Oracles wee need,
To bee inform'd of things that ſhall ſucceed:
No Oracle of Delphos, *but of* Sion,
No booke, but that of God, muſt wee relie on.

No

No Starre, but Jacobs *Starre, can doe the feate,*
To end our woes, and make our joyes compleate.

   Could I th' harmonious forrowes parallel
   Of the incefted mournfull Philomel :
   Or could I imitate that fatall note,
   Which is effufed from the filver throte
   Of that faire Bird, y' cleapt Apollo's *Prieft,*
   Who clad in feather'd Albe, with his foft breft
   Divides the furface of the cryftall ftream,
   And dying fings his owne fad requiem ;
   Then might I fuch fad Elegies devife,
   As would become our mournfull tragedies.
   But give mee leave a fpace for to difmiffe
   Melpomene, *and bloudy* Nemefis,
   And to elect a ftyle which may appeare
   More mild to many, though to fome fevere.

Learned

LEarn'd *Scaliger*, the fecond of the twaine,
Second to none in Arts, did late complaine
To *wife Apollo*, of fome ftrange abufes,
Committed againft him and the *Nine Mufes*:
For *Scaliger* had beene *Grave Cenfour* long,
In *Learnings Commonwealth*, and liv'd among
The people of *Parnaffus*, in fuch fame,
That all the world tooke notice of his name :
Himfelfe hee humbly to his Lord addreft,
And in thefe termes, his inward thoughts expreft.
(Dread Prince) to whofe benevolous afpect
Wee owe our Arts, and Hearts, with all refpect
Which may bee due unto a Soveraigne Lord,
Who rules by Love, and Law, not by the Sword ;
I, whom your *Majefty* daign'd to create
Cenfour of manners, in the *Learned State*,
Obliged by the dutie of my place,
Humbly prefume to importune your Grace,
Unto my votes to adde your royall will,
For a redreffe of fome abufes ill.

Needs

Needs muſt wee thoſe advantages confeſſe,
Which wee reape from the literary Preſſe,
A priviledge which our forefathers wanted,
Although to us Heaven it benignely granted :
This engine of the *Muſes* doth diſperſe
Arts beſt achievements, both in Proſe and Verſe :
It vents with eaſe, labours of learned braines,
And doth the hand quit from a world of paines :
Thoſe *Wonders*, of which elder ages boaſt,
Had almoſt all forgotten been, and loſt,
If this *Eighth Wonder* had not been contriv'd,
Whereby the other ſeven have been reviv'd.
Your Grace well knowes (I need not to relate)
How *Typographie* doth concerne your ſtate,
Which ſome pernicious heads have ſo abus'd,
That many wiſh it never had been us'd :
This inſtrument of Art, is now poſſeſt
By ſome, who have in Art no intereſt ;
For it is now imploy'd by Paper-waſters,
By mercenary ſoules, and Poëtaſters,
Who weekly utter, ſlanders, libells, lies,
Under the name of ſpecious novelties :
Thus *Captaine Raſhingham's* undone, and loſt,
For theſe his trade and cuſtome have engroſt :

And

And Hee, (for to maintaine an honeſt port)
Is forc'd t' accept an office in your Court;
Hee in your Graces kitchin plucks the Widgeons,
Geeſe, Dotterells, and Duckes, and all tame Pidgeons,
And for his labour hee their plums retaines,
Wages, that ſute his perſon, and his paines;
But let not your *High Majeſty* miſtake,
And thinke that my complaint is for his ſake :
If this abuſe touch'd onely ſuch as hee,
It were no grievance, but a remedy :
For *Truth*, and *Morall Vertues* injur'd are;
The *Muſes*, and the *Graces* beare a ſhare,
In theſe notorious wrongs, with all that love
Parnaſſus, or the *Heliconian Grove* :
Therefore (*Great Prince*) vouchſafe for to apply
Your Soveraigne power, and authority,
To vindicate your ſubjects, and to curbe
Thoſe Varlets, that your government diſturbe.
Thus ſpake the *Cenſour*, then *Apollo* ſhook
His harniſh'd lockes, and with a frowning look,
Declar'd his diſcontent; but having paus'd,
Hee thus reply'd : *Grave Cenſour* I'm amaz'd,
To heare the impudent affronts of theſe
That thus contemne our Lawes, and our decrees,

B   But

But (by this golden Scepter) they fhall try
What 'tis to trefpaffe on our lenity :
If our remifneffe hath made them tranfgreffe,
They fhall perceive that wee can make it leffe,
In their fharpe punifhment. Thus *Phœbus* ends,
And then Hee for *Torquato Taſſo* fends ;
Under whofe charge fome Companies were lifted
Of that ftout Gend'army, which confifted
Of Heroick Poets, whofe high valour was,
No meane defenfe, but a magnifick grace
Unto the Sacred Hill : this Regiment,
On fummons fhort, was ever ready bent
To execute *Apollo's* juft commands,
With hearts couragious, and with armed hands.
Stout *Taſſo* did in fturdy buffe appeare,
And after reverence done, defir'd to heare
His Graces pleafure ; who foone gave him orders,
With all his Cavalry, to fcoure the borders
Of high *Parnaſſus*, and low *Helicon*,
And to bring in alive, or dead, each one
That had difcovered been, or to defile
The Preffe with Pamphlets fcarrilous, and vile,
Or to have traduc'd with malignant fpirits,
Perfons of honorable worth, and merits.

Taſſo

Taſſo departs with theſe inſtruⅽtions,
And muſter'd up his witty *Myrmidons* :
The trumpet to the ſtirrop gives a call :
They buſtle to their armes, and mounted all,
Haſte to their Rendezvous without delay,
And put in ranke, and file, they march away :
For *Taſſo* no advantage did decline,
To proſecute the better his deſigne ;
Hee into ſquadrons three his Troopes diſſeⅽts,
And unto ſeverall quarters them direⅽts,
That traverſing the countrey round about,
They might the ſooner find theſe foxes out ;
In each ſuſpicious angle *Taſſo* ſeekes,
And in this inquiſition ſpent ſome weekes :
Nor did his other parties with negleⅽt
Performe what they injoyn'd were to effeⅽt ;
The limits of *Parnaſſus* they ſurround,
And *Helicon*, with verdant Laurells crown'd :
Mount *Pindus*, and thoſe valleys ever greene
Where pale *Pyrene*, and pure *Hippocrene*
In liquid cryſtall rife, they ſearch'd throughout ;
Nor was the Vale of *Tempe* left unſought :
Nor did their labours miſſe ſucceſſe deſir'd :
For they, before a moneth was full expir'd,

B 2   Had

Had clear'd the coaſts, and many pris'ners gain'd ;
Which malefactors they in chaines detain'd,
And them convey'd unto *Apolloes* Court,
Who welcom'd *Taſſo* in moſt gratious ſort :
And for his faithfull ſervice, him hee made
Lieutenant Generall of that proud Brigade
Of the Italian Poets : This reward
Made elder *Dante*, and *Petrarch* to regard
His dignitie with ill affected eyes :
And *Arioſto* diſcontent likewiſe :
But *Phœbus* did brave *Taſſo's* merit weigh
By reaſon, but in ſcales of paſſion they ;
And when hee did perceive that they did fret,
To ſee themſelves behind their Junior ſet,
Hee them aſſur'd they muſt expect t' inherit
Parnaſſus honours not by time, but merit.
But when *Apollo* with his radiant looke
The Pris'ners had into amazement ſtrooke,
Hee cauſ'd thoſe guiltie ſoules to bee convey'd
To the *Trophonian denne*, there to bee laid
In Irons cold, untill they ſhould bee brought
To tryall for thoſe miſchiefs they had wrought.
Apollo then a ſolemne ſummons ſent
To all thoſe honour'd Peers that did frequent

The

The Learned Hill, and ftrictly them injoyn'd,
Him to attend, upon a day affign'd :
For in a full *Afsife* hee did intend
The crimes of thefe delinquents to perpend :
His loyall Nobles fail'd not, to refort
(Without delay) unto their Soveraignes Court,
And on the day, which was for judgement fet,
They all in the Prætorian hall were met :
Where *Phœbus,* on his high tribunall fate,
With his *Affeffours,* in triumphant ftate ;
Sage *Verulam* fublim'd for fcience great,
As *Chancellour,* next him had the firft feat :
And next to him, *Budeus* did appear,
Hee of *Parnaffus* was *High Treafurer :*
Sidney tooke place upon the other fide,
Who th' office of *High Conftable* fupply'd :
But *Picus* of *Mirandula,* (who was
High Chamberlaine) affumed the fourth place ;
The elder *Scaliger* his place then tooke
Before *Erafmus,* who fhew'd in his looke
Diftafte, for hee (like *Pompey*) tooke difpleafure
To fee himfelfe put downe by *Julius Cefar.*
In cuerpo then did *Juftus Lipfius* fit,
Who more devotion had expreft then wit,

When

When to an *Image* hee bequeath'd his gown ;
But had hee not been for a *Turncoate* known,
His offer'd garment might have found efteeme,
Which fitter for a Frippery did feeme,
Then for her ufe, to whom it was prefented.
Next him fate *Barclay*, fomewhat difcontented,
'Caufe hee had fail'd in finding that refpect,
Which hee from *Romes Archflamen* did expect.
Bodine, Turnebus, Cafaubon and *Grotius,*
Mafcardus, Heinfius, Selden, Vofsius,
Approved Criticks all, did there appeare
On the judiciall Bench with lookes fevere.
But when old *Camden* thought to take his place,
Apollo him repuls'd with fome difgrace :
For hee of late receiv'd had a complaint
From hands of credit, which did him attaint
Of mifdemeanours, acted in a ftory,
That did detract from a *Great Ladies* glory,
Wherein hee was accus'd to have reveal'd
Some things, which better might have been conceal'd
Had they been truths : What madneffe him mifled,
T'afperfe the afhes of that *Phœnix* dead,
With notes of infamy, whofe fun'rall flame
Ravifh'd the world with th'odour of her fame ?

Doubt-

Doubtleffe the living hee to flatter knew,
Much better then to give the dead her due.
  (The Court thus fet) the fturdy *Keeper* then
Of the unhofpitall *Trophonian Den*,
His trembling Pris'ners brought unto the barre ;
For fterne afpect, with *Mars* hee might compare,
But by his belly, and his double chinne,
Hee look'd like the old Hofte of a *New Inne*.
Thus when fowre *Ben* his fetter'd cattell had
Shut up together in the pinfold fad :
John Taylour, then the Courts fhrill *Chanticleere*,
Did fummon all the *Furours* to appeare :
Hee had the Cryers place : an office fit,
For him that hath a better voyce, then wit.
Hee, who was called firft in all the Lift,
George Withers hight, entitled Satyrift ;
Then *Cary, May*, and *Davenant* were call'd forth ;
Renowned Poets all, and men of worth,
If wit may paffe for worth. Then *Sylvefter,*
Sands, Drayton, Beaumont, Fletcher, Mafsinger,
Shakefpeare, and *Heywood*, Poets good and free ;
Dramatick writers all, but the firft three :
Thefe were empanell'd all, and being fworne
A juft and perfect verdict to returne,

A

A Malefactour then receiv'd command,
Before the Barre to elevate his hand;
Mercurius Britanicus by name,
Was hee, who firft was call'd to play his game :
Then *Edmund Spenfer* Clarke of the Affife,
Read the Endictment loud, which did comprife
Matters of fcandall, and contempt extreme,
Done 'gainft the Dignitie, and Diademe
Of great *Apollo*, and that legall courfe,
Which throughout all *Parnaffus* was in force.
For ufe of Mercury hee was accuf'd,
Which weekely hee into his inke infuf'd,
Thereby to murther, and deftroy the fame
Of many, with ftrange obloquie, and fhame.
Hee likewife was accuf'd, to have purloin'd
Some drachmes of wit, with a felonious mind,
From *Helicon*, which hee in Satyrs mixt,
To make fome laugh, and others deepely vext.
Unto his charge they likewife did object,
That when hee faw his lines could not effect
His ends, and aymes, which were his foe to kill,
Or elfe to make him throw away his quill;
That then hee fought by magick Arts to call
Archilochus his ghoft from *Pluto's* hall,

To

To teach him how fuch language to indite,
As might make fome even hang themfelves for fpite.
  This was his charge in brief; (which being read)
  To his indictment he was call'd to plead :
Not guilty, he replies, and did fubmit
Himfelfe to the integrity and wit
Of twelve fufficient Poets, but entreated,
To heare the Jurours names againe repeated :
(Which done) hee on exceptions did infift,
Afferted againft divers of the lift.
On confident *George Withers* firft hee fix'd,
As one unfit with others to bee mix'd
In his arraignment, for he did proteft,
That *Withers* was a cruell Satyrift ;
And guilty of the fame offence and crime,
Whereof hee was accufed at this time :
Therefore for him hee thought it fitter farre,
To ftand as a Delinquent at the barre,
Then to bee now empanell'd in a Jury.
George Withers then, with a Poetick fury,
Began to blufter, but *Apollo's* frowne
Made him forbeare, and lay his choler downe.
But *Phœbus*, thus *Britanicus* corrects,
Our Majefty (faid hee) which ftill protects

        C   The

The innocent, but doth offendours fcourge,
Ingag'd is honeft *Withers* for to purge
From this offence : for his impartiall pen
Did rather groffe abufes taxe, then men :
Or that hee did tranfgreffe, let us admit ;
Since long agoe, hee fmarted for his wit.
Nor was *Britanicus* with this abafh'd,
For with his cavils hee fought to have dafh'd
Two other able Jurours, and thefe were
Deferving *Sands* and gentle *Sylvefter :*
To thefe opprobious language hee affords,
And them Tranflators call'd, and men of words,
No Poets, but meer Rhymers, for (faid hee)
Invention is the foule of poefie,
And who can fay, that fuch a foule as this,
Is to bee found in their abilities ?
For thefe are bondmen to anothers ftile,
And when they have beftow'd much time, and toile,
They doe but what, before, was better done ;
For Poemes lofe by their tranflation,
And are deprived of that luftre brave,
Which their originalls are wont to have :
Yea all the workes of thefe Tranflators vaine,
Are rather labour of the hand, then braine :

Their

Their afinine endeavours have effected,
That nobler tongues and arts are now neglected ;
While they in vulgar language reprefent
Thofe notions which from vulgar wits diffent :
This knot of Knaves the Common-wealth afflicts
Of your *Parnafsus* with their jugling tricks ;
For Rubies which in gold at firft were fet,
They into copper put, whereby they cheat
The fimpler fort, that want a piercing eye,
The difference of metals to defcry.
Thus fpake *Britanicus* : while many fmil'd ;
But *Sands* look'd pale, and *Sylvefter* wax'd wild
For anger and difdaine ; *Apollo* then
Thus interpos'd, to vindicate thefe men,
Britanicus (faid hee) we have too long
The language heard of thy traducing tongue,
But *Syluefters*, and *Sands* his worth is fuch,
That thy reproach cannot their honour touch :
Since Kings for Majefty, and arts renown'd,
Have with receptions kind, their labours crown'd.
Befides, wee are inclin'd by fome refpects,
Challeng'd from us, by the infirmer fex,
Thefe writers of *Parnaffus* to fupport,
To pleafe the fancy of that female fort,

C 2

Whom

Whom want of thefe tranflations might fpurre on,
For to acquire, and get more tongues then one :
Which if they fhould accomplifh, men might rue
Thofe mifchiefes which would thereupon enfue.
But if nor *Sands*, nor *Sylvefter* can merit,
The titles of true Poets to inherit,
For what they have perform'd, yet wee relie
So much upon their truth, and loyaltie,
That wee caufe them to paffe upon thy tryall,
In fpite of thy exception or denyall.
Thus fpake *Apollo :* then the Pris'ner was
Injoyn'd to ftand afide, and in his place
Did *Aulicus* fucceed, who by command,
In humble fort uprear'd his guilty hand :
Full fadly his indictment he attends,
Which him impeach'd, that hee for wicked ends
Had the *Caftalian Spring* defil'd with gall ;
And chang'd by witchcraft, moft Satyricall,
The bayes of *Helicon*, and myrtles mild,
To pricking hauthornes, and to hollyes wild.
Hee was accus'd, that he with flanders falfe,
With forged fictions, calumnies and tales,
Had fought the *Spartane Ephori* to fhame,
And added fewell to the direfull flame

Of

Of civill difcord, and domefticke blowes,
By the incentives of malicious profe.
For whereas, hee fhould have compos'd his inke
Of liquours, that make flames expire, and fhrinke
Into their cinders, it was there objected,
That hee had his of burning oile confected,
Of Naphtha, Gunpowder, Pitch, and Saltpeter,
Which thofe combuftions raifed, and made greater.
Hee was accus'd to have unjuftly ftung
The fage *Amphictyons* with his venom'd tongue ;
And that he like the fierce Albanian curre,
Did ftubbornly choofe rather to demurre,
And bee difmembred by anothers wit,
Then loofe his teeth from thofe, whom firft hee bit.
Hee was accus'd, that he had us'd his skill,
Parnaffus with ftrange herefies to fill,
And that he labour'd had for to bring in,
Th' exploded doctrines of the *Florentine*,
And taught that to diffemble and to lie,
Where vitall parts of humane policie :
Of his endictment this was the full fenfe :
To which the Pris'ner pleades his innocence,
And puts himfelfe upon a legall tryall,
But he withall exhibites a denyall

C 3

Againft

Againſt a Jurour, for his ſuit it was,
That *May* on his arraignment might not paſſe :
For though a Poet hee muſt him confeſſe,
Becauſe his writings did atteſt no leſſe ;
Yet hee deſir'd hee might be ſet aſide,
Becauſe hee durſt not in his truth confide :
Of *May* among twelve moneths he well approv'd,
But *May* among Twelve men hee never lov'd :
For hee beleev'd that out of private ſpite
Hee would his conſcience ſtraine, t' undoe him quite.
Hee likewiſe of offences him accus'd,
Whereby his King *Apollo* was abus'd :
And with malicious arguments attempts
To prove him guilty of ſublime contempts,
But chiefly he indeavour'd to conclude,
That hee was guilty of ingratitude :
Which crime *Parnaſſus* Lawes doe ſo oppoſe,
As in that State, it for high Treaſon goes.
   Then *May* ſtept forth, and firſt implor'd the grace
   And leave of *Phœbus* to maintaine his caſe :
Then to the *Learned Cunſiſtory* ſues,
That they would him or cenſure, or excuſe :
Then calls the Gods, and all whom they protect,
The Starres, and all on whom they doe reflect,
The

The Elements, and what's compos'd of thefe,
Him to acquit from all difloyalties.
If by juft proofes (faid hee) thou canft evince,
That I have beene ungratefull to my Prince,
Then let mee from thefe groves bee now exil'd
To Scythian fnowes, or into deferts wild ;
Yea, I invoke the Gods that I may feele
The Gyants valour, or *Ixions* wheele,
If it bee found I have tranfgreffed thus,
As 'tis inform'd by lying *Aulicus.*
Apollo then darts forth an awfull ray
From his impiercing eye, which filenc'd *May.*
So *Kings* (if they bee juft) may rule like Gods,
And be obferved by their lookes, and nods.
Hee *Aulicus* rebuk'd, becaufe hee knew
His accufation from meere malice grew :
And him advis'd in peace to ftand afide,
If hee defir'd with favour to be try'd.
The *Cryer* then did fummon to the Bar,
The *Penman* of the *Weekely Calendar,*
Entituled the new *Ephemerides,*
Perfeſt Diurnalls call them, if you pleafe ;
But their perfeſtion cannot mee invite,
To thinke they merit fuch an Epethite,

                                         Except

Except truths now for imperfections paffe,
And gold in eftimation yeelds to braffe.
   Of his endictment the whole fumme was this,
   That hee had wrong'd th' *Athenian Novelifts*,
By felling them meere aire, in ftead of Sack,
And puffes of wind, for ftrong Frontigniac :
For empty bottles hee was wont to mixe
Among full flafques, and with thefe cheating trickes
Deceiv'd thofe Merchants, who were not fo wife
To know the full from empty by the poife.
A fourth Delinquent then was called out,
A *Second Proteus* or the learned *Scout* :
This wife *Chamæleon* was wont to weare
That hue, which was propounded by his feare :
The fumme of his indictment this contain'd ;
That whereas hee had from *Apollo* gain'd
A *Patent* to report true newes abroad,
Without diffimulation, guile, or fraud,
Yet hee adulterated had his ware
With manifold impertinences rare
Yea from his center fwarv'd, and gone aftray
Into fome matters farre beyond his way :
And that hee with eight *Pages undifcret*,
Had tofs'd and tax'd high actions in a fheet :
That

That he prognofticks had prefum'd to reare,
On ftarres above his quadrant, and his fpheare :
And that he had prefum'd likewife to mixe
With his Avifoes fweet, foure politicks,
Difperfing weekly maximes of State,
As if he chiefly at the helme had fate :
And that he had oft in ambiguous fafhions,
Appear'd as one transform'd in his relations,
That it was very difficult to find,
Whether he were a bird, or beaft by kind :
He was accus'd, that he with cenfures bold,
The actions of his betters had controld,
And that he with his mercenary hand,
Had touch'd affaires of weight not to be fcann'd
By fuch as hee : thus was the *Scout* indited,
But when he was unto his anfwer cited,
Hee pleads himfelfe to be an Innocent,
And humbly crav'd the *Bench* for to confent
To his impunity, and to difpence
VVith errours, that arife from indigence :
He further added ; fince his fate it was
To be referr'd for tryall of his cafe
Unto twelve mouthes ; he crav'd they would admit
Twelve nofes too ; him to condemne, or quit,

D That

That no defect might be of any fence,
To fmell, or to find out his innocence.
Apollo then retorts an irefull glance,
And dafh'd the Pris'ner out of countenance :
He told him now 't was time to lay afide
Impertinent difcourfe, he fhould be tryd
By twelve, who were fufficient Men, and fit
Both for integrity, and pregnant wit :
And as for him, whofe Vote he did reject,
Upon a cavill againft fome defect :
Hee him affur'd that all the world might know,
His art was high, although his nofe was low :
But *Madagafcar* chiefly did exprefs
His raptures brave, and laur'ate worthinefs.
The *Scout* commanded was then to ftand by :
And *Civicus* held up his hand on high :
Good civill *Civicus*, who to his booke
Emblemes affix'd, of what he undertooke,
For filly rimes appear'd in the firft place,
To which was added fome Commanders face,
That in refemblance, did no more comply
With him, whom it was faid to fignifie,
Then doe fome ftoryes which his books containe,
Refemble truths : But his offences vaine,

In

In his endictment were declar'd at large,
And this was the full purport of his charge;
He was accus'd that he through fcience bad,
Or Magick, or Magnetick figures, had
Prefixed to his books; which did enchant
The fancies of the weak, and ignorant,
And caus'd them to beftow more time, and coine,
On fuch fond Pamphlets, then on books divine :
It was affirm'd, that he was wont to fcatter,
Upon his fingle fheet, more words, then matter,
And that he had with tranfmarine narrations,
Recruted his domefticall relations,   (courfe
And from the *Danes* and *Swedes* fetch'd cold dif-
To cloy the ftomacks of his Auditours ;
And with fuch ftuffe his latter pages patch'd,
That they *Brittannicus* his doctrines match'd,
Who doubts, and fatisfactions wont t'invent,
That gave nor fatisfaction nor content.
VVhile *Civicus* did thus his tryall heare ;
One comes, and whifpers *Phœbus* in the eare,
And him advertis'd, that a fecret friend
Of *Civicus*, did to his *Highnefs* fend,
A prefent of fome Sack, and fugar loaves,
And that therewith, the Giver humbly moves,

D 2   That

That the poore Pris'ner might receive fuch grace,
As might be juftly found in fuch a cafe.
Apollo then, in choler and difdain,
Did thus break out in termes. VVhat madnefs vain,
Or impudence (faid He) in humane race   (face
Remains ?   That they fhould think with bribes t'ef-
Our refolutions juft, and us divert
From judgement by the law, and by defert ;
Then he the *Gaoler* call'd for (*Honeft Ben*)
The Keeper fat, of the *Trophonian Den* :
Him he commands to feize upon (in haft)
The bringer of the bribe, and keep him faft ;
And fince the *Tubbe* of which he told the tale,
By fplitting, had deceiv'd him of his ale ;
And fince his *New-Inne* too had got a crack,
He bids him take the Sugar loves, and Sack,
To make his lov'd *Magnatick Lady* glad,
That ftill (for want of an applaufe) was fad.
    Then *Civicus* unto his charge did plead
Not guilty, and was bidden to recede.
    Then with a look like to his ftyle fubmiffe,
Stood forth. the *Writer* of *Occurrences* :
He was accufed to have injur'd *Fame*,
And to have difguis'd falfhood by the name

                                                    Of

Of *Truth*, and with a goodly *Frontifpeice*,
To have procur'd his bookes efteeme, and price :
Which were compar'd unto a painted Inne,
That had nor good wine, nor good cheare within.
He was accus'd, that like a fubtile theife,
He had his readers rob'd of their beleife,
And of their wit, and judgment them bereav'd,
That willingly, were with his lies deceiv'd :
But if fome truths (by chance) he utter'd had,
Thefe were in fuch a tedious language clad,
That many actors of renowned jefts,
Depriv'd were of their honor'd interefts,
By his inglorious penne, and alfo thofe
Who did affect true elegance in profe,
Did from his ruftick phrafe conceive more hate,
Then pleafure from thofe things he did relate.
It likewife was deliver'd in his charge,
That he had tortur'd, with his letters large,
Ingenious eares, which to plebeian hands
He captives made, in aufcultations bands.
And that mens names, on credit he up tooke,
All which he lifted to fill up his booke,
And for to make a greater noife, he fummes
Both Trumpets, Seargeants, Corporalls, & drums,

D 3

Among

Among the numbers of the flain, or taken,
Wherby he did great Officers awaken,
That flep't in honours bed, who did complaine,
To fee themfelves mixt with that vulgar train
    The Pris'ners plea to this indictment was
Flat negative, for in the plaineft cafe,
Al Malefactors hate confeffion free ;
Confeffe and hang is ftill their maximè.
The Pris'ner alfo crav'd, he might be heard,
While he againft a jury-man preferr'd
A juft exception, his requeft was granted,
And fraught with malice, though much wit he
He gentle Mr. *Cary* did refufe,   (wanted,
Who pleas'd faire Ladies with his courtly mufe :
He faid, that he by his luxurious penne,
Deferv'd had better the *Trophonian Denne*,
Then many now which ftood to be arraign'd,
For he the *Thefpian Fountaine* had diftain'd,
With foule conceits, and made their waters bright,
Impure, like thofe of the *Hermophrodite*,
He faid, that he in verfe, more loofe had bin,
Then old *Chærephanes*, or *Aretine*,
In obfcæne portraitures : and that this fellow
In *Helicon* had reard the firft *Burdello*,

                      That

That he had chang'd the chaft *Caftalian fpring*,
Into a *Carian Well*, whofe waters bring
Effeminate defires, and thoughts uncleane,
To minds that earft were pure, and moft ferene,
Thus fpake the pris'ner, when a furious glance,
Was darted from *Apollos* countenance,
Which ftrook him dumb : then *Scaliger the wife*
Was call'd, to whom A*pollo* thus aplies
His Speech. *Grave Cenfour* of our learned Hill
Whom your owne merit, and our royall will
Hath fupervifour made of Arts, and Mufes,
I wonder at the noife of thefe abufes,
For I conceive not yet, that thefe effects,
Should be th'unhappy fruites of your neglects,
So well you'ave purg'd the *errours of the Times*,
That I think not you could permit fuch crimes,
Our manners to corrupt, fince that our fprings
Ought to be kept as pure as beds of Kings :
For he that vice, with fcience doth commixe,
Turnes noble *Hippocren'* to ugly *Styx*,
In marriage bonds hoth Heaven and Hell combine
Yet Art may Heaven and earth together joyne :
Thus fpake *Apollo*, then learn'd *Scaliger*
Shap'd the replye : I have (my Soveraigne deare)
With

With care intended what concerns my place,
So to conferve your fprings from mixtures bafe,
Yet all my care, and labour is but vaine,
Except *Jove* will confent t'undoe againe
His worke of H*umane nature*, and the fame
Of fuch pure ftuffe, and perfect temper frame,
As it of no corruption may admit :
For I have try'd my induftry and wit,
Both Arts, and Authours to refine, and mend,
As well as times, yet can I not defend,
But fome luxuriant witt, will often vent
Lafcivious Poëms, againft my confent :
Of which offence, if *Cary* guilty be,
Yet may fome chafter Songs him render free
From cenfure fharp, and expiate thofe crimes
Which are not fully his, but rather Times :
But let your Grace vouchfafe, that he may try
How he can make his own Apology :
Apollo then gave *Cary* leave to fpeake,
Who thus in modeft fort, did filence breake.

In wifdomes nonage, and unriper yeares,
Some lines flipt from my penne, which fince with
I labour'd to expunge : This Song of mine   (teares
Was not infufed by the Virgins nine,

Nor

Nor through my dreames divine upon this Hill,
Did this vain *Rapture* iſſue from my quill,
No Theſpian waters, but a Paphian fire,
Did me with this foule extaſie inſpire :
I oft have wiſh'd, that I (like *Saturne*) might
This Infant of my folly ſmother quite,
Or that I could retract, what I had done,
Into the boſome of Oblivion.
Thus *Cary* did conclude : for preſt by griefe,
Hee was compell'd to be conciſe, and briefe :
Phœbus at his contrition did relent,
And Edicts ſo on through all *Parnaſſus* ſent,
That none ſhould dare to attribute the ſhame
Of that fond *rapture*, unto *Caryes* name,
But Order'd that the infamy ſhould light
On thoſe, who did the ſame read, or recite.
Hee further-more the Pris'ner did injoyne,
Againſt him all exceptions to decline,
And to a legall tryall for to ſtand,
If Hee expected favour at his hand.
  The innocent *Scotch Dove* did then advance,
Full ſober in his wit, and countenance,
And though his books contain'd not mickle ſence,
Yet his endictment ſhew'd no great offence ;

E

Great

Great Wits, to perills great themfelves expofe
Oft'times; but the *Scotch Dove* was none of thofe :
In many words he little matter dreft,
And did Laconick brevity deteft,
Perfpicuous phrafe he lov'd, could not endure
To be in ftile, or in his life obfcure,
But while his Readers did expect fome newes,
They found a Sermon, thus did he abufe
Good people, that he rather might have took
A Lapwing, then a Dove to trimme a book :
   This was his charge : and being call'd to plead,
   Hee cryes not guilty, and petitioned
He might be heard to vindicate his worth
From fcandall, and reproach, on him caft forth
By *Aulicus*, that fcoffing *Hipponax*,
Who with lewd crimes, did him unjuftly tax ;
His fute was granted, then did he complaine
That *Aulicus*, his title did difdaine,
And fpitefully in ftead of *Scottifh Pigeon*,
Had him the nick-name given of *Scottifh Wigion*
And that he had moft falfly him accus'd,
Preftigious Arts, and Magick to have us'd,
Whereby Mens fenfes were with errours ftrook,
That firebrands, they for *Olive branches* took.
Thus

Thus fpake the *Dove*: *Apollo* then reply'd,
Wee might condemne your arrogance, and pride,
'Caufe you the name of *Venus* birds have chofe,
When *Scotland* hath (you know) no birds like thofe,
Though it abounds with fowle of various kinds;
But errours fmall provoke not heavenly minds,
I doubt not, but that *Aulicus* his tongue
Hath injur'd you, but were this all the wrong
Which it hath done, He might our cenfure fcape,
And paffe, not for a Serpent, but an Ape.
Thus *Phœbus* fpake; And then the *Scottifh* Dove
Rejoyn'd, as zeale and choler did him move;

I challenge to the duell of the pen
Falfe *Aulicus*, that Cynick among men,
That enemy of Truth, true honours fcourge,
That Officine of lyes, and flanders forge,
Oh let your Grace vouchfafe to turne me loofe,
A *Scottifh* Dove, againft the *Romifh Goofe.*
Apollo then reflects a frowning eye,
Commands him to defift, and to ftand by.

The *Cryer* then did the fwift *Poft* command,
At his indictment to hold up his hand:
He was accus'd of thefe enormities,
Firft that with Encheridions of lyes,

E 2   Hee

He had difturb'd the learned Common-weale,
And alfo in felonious fort did fteale
From *Euphues*, and *Arcadia*, language gay
Therein his vain relations to array,
Becaufe he knew that lyes in fine attires,
Preferr'd are before truths, by many buyers :
Such was his ftyle, fuch tales did he endite,
That he no newes, but *Romants* feem'd to write ;
It alfo ftrongly was againft him urg'd,
That he fome Packets had contriv'd, and forg'd,
Which letters did of falfe reports containe,
And this was meerely done for thirft of gaine :
This was his charge ; and becaufe he divin'd
That free confeffion might fome favour find,
Hee guilty pleads, and then was fet afide.
Another then was call'd forth to be try'd :
And this was he, who weekly did difpence
A mifcellany of intelligence :
Of his endictment, the effect was this,
That he had with his weekly rapfodyes,
The Affes of *Parnafsus* fore annoy'd,
Whom he had fed with many rumours voyd,
And vapours vain.   Thus like Chamelions they
Took fmoke in ftead of provender and hay,

And

And therby grew in fence fo leane, and lame :
That quite unfit for fervice they became ;
It was alleadg'd, that he for lucres fake,
Did falfe intelligence devife, and make,
And car'd not who he gul'd, or did beguile,
Soe he might reap therby fome profit vile.

Thefe were the crimes, wherof he was accus'd
To which he pleads not guilty, but refus'd
By Hiftriomicke Poëts to be try'd,
'Gainft whom, he thus malicioufly enveigh'd
    Juftice (fayd he) and no finifter fury,
    Difwades me from a tryall by a jury,
That of worfe mifdemeanours guilty bee,
Then thofe which are objected againft mee :
Thefe mercinary pen-men of the Stage,
That fofter the grand vifes of this age,
Should in this Common-wealth no office beare,
But rather ftand with vs Delinquents here :
Shakefpear's a Mimicke, *Maffinger* a Sot,
H*eywood* for *Aganippe* takes a plot :
Beamount and *Fletcher* make one poët, they
Single, dare not adventure on a Play.
Thefe things are all but th'errour of the Mufes,
Abortive witts, foul fountains of abufes :

E 3   Reptiles

Reptiles, which are equivocally bred,
Under fome hedge, not in that geniall bed
Where lovely art with a brave wit conjoyn'd,
Engenders Poëts of the nobleſt kind.
Plato refus'd ſuch creatures to admit
Into his Common-wealth, and is it fit
Parnaſſus ſhould the exiles entertaine
Of *Plato* ? therefore (my dread Soveraigne)
I crave your Pardon, while I thus preſume
To ſupplicate your Highneſs, to reſume
Your wonted Juſtice, that this ſacred Hill,
No more may ſuffer by ſuch members ill ;
Thus ſpake the Pris'ner : then among the crowd,
Plautus, and *Terence* 'gan to mutter loud,
And old *Menander* was but ill apayd,
While *Ariſtophanes* his wrath bewray'd,   (ly,
With words opprobr'ous ; for it gall'd him ſhrewd-
To ſee dramatick Poets tax'd ſo lewdly :
And while 'mongſt theſe, the murmure did encreaſe,
The Cryer warn'd them all to hold their peace.
  The Court was ſilent, then *Apollo* ſpake :
If thou (ſaid He) chiefly for vertues ſake,
Or true affection to the Common-weale,
Didſt our Dramatick Poëts thus appeale,
                                        VVe

VVe fhould to thy exception give confent,
But fince we are affur'd, 'tis thy intent,
By this refufall, onely to deferre
That cenfure, which our juftice muft conferre
Upon thy merizs ; we muft needs decline
From approbation of thefe pleas of thine,
And are refolv'd that at this time, and place,
They fhall as Jurours, on thy tryall paffe,
But if our *Cenfour*, fhall hereafter find,
They have deferved ill, we have defign'd
That they likewife fhall be to judgement brought,
To fuffer for thofe crimes, which they have wrought,
Thus fpake the Soveraign of the two-topp'd Mount,
Another then was call'd to an account,
And this was he, who weekly did pretend,
Accounts of certain news abroad to fend.
He was accus'd, that he with Pamphlets vain,
The art of lying had fought to maintain,
VVhich trade, he and his fellows us'd of late,
VVith fuch fucceffe, and profit in the State
Of high *Parnaffus*, that they did confpire,
A *Patent* from *Apollo* to acquire :
That they might thus incorporated bee,
Into a *Company* of *Lyers free*.

This

This was his charge : while he no whit relents,
But ftood to juftifie his innocence.
The *Pen-man* of the *Perfeƈt Paſsages*
Then to his tryall did himfelfe addreffe,
He was accus'd, that he for love of gain,
Had injur'd Truth, with many ftories vain,
And that Hee with his mercenary quill,
Difhonour'd had A*pollo's Noble Hill.*
That Hee, and his affociates had attempted
In a felonious manner, to have empty'd
The Fountaines of the Mufes, to fulfill
That appetite which rofe from *Livers ill.*
   To this indiƈtment he gave a denyall,
    And yeelds himfelfe fubmiffively to his tryall.
The fubtile *Spye* then to the barre drew nere,
And with dejeƈted lookes, his hand did reare :
But he in his indiƈtment was accus'd,
Old Galilæos glaſses to have us'd,
Which reprefented objeƈts to his eye,
Beyond their meafure, and juft fymmetrie,
VVhereby the faults of many did appeare,
More and farre greater, then indeed they were :
And that he at a diftance did recount,
(Like *Lynceus* from the Lilybean mount)

Numbers

Numbers of fhipps and men, though he indeed
So blind was, that he did a leader need.
He was accus'd that (like *Aglaures*) hee
Forbidden objects had prefum'd to fee,
And therefore merited in law, and fence,
His eares to forfeit, for his eyes offence.

   Thus his Indictment rann : It he denies,
   And for a tryall, on twelve men relyes ;
But this defpitefull *Spye* a cavill rais'd
'Gainft *Michael Drayton*, whom he much difprais'd
For that great *Poly-Olbion* which he writ,
This he tearm'd a rude Embrion of wit,
Apeice of low efteeme, together layd
Without propicious *Pallas*, or the ayde
Of the nine Mufes, who did much difdaine
The homely features cf his *Naiad's* vaine.

   Thus fpake the *Spye*, and ftill would have pro-
If that A*pollo* had not him impeded.   (ceeded

   I thinke through th'infolence of thefe (faid hee)
And our remiffneffe : we this Barr fhall fee
Become a ftage of the *Old Comedye*,

   How boldly hath this proud traduceing *Spye*,
And his *Comrades*, our honeft Poëts checkt,
Who from the beft have ever found refpect :

F

Nor

Nor can fmooth *Drayton* fcape their cenfures fharp
But at his workes this bufy *Spye* muft carp :
Drayton, whofe Sonnets fweet of *Love heroicke*
May melt th'*Effæan,* or the *rigid Stoicke*
To amorous *Leanders,* and them move
Through Seas of teares, to fwim to her they love.
This *Swanne* of ours, that impure *Zoylus* blots
With fcandalls foule, but as the *Ermines* fpotts
Adde price and eftimation to his Furre,
Soe the reproofes of this invective curre
Give light, and luftre unto *Draytons* worth,
And with advantage fet his merit forth :
Drayton, who doth, in fuch magnificke fort
Delineate Valour in his *Agincourte,*
That this illuftr'ous poëme, doth infpire
Even courages of ice, with warlike fire.
His *Tragicke Legends* are with force endu'd,
To foften Scythyans, and Tartars rude,
Yea with pathetick Fancies to enchant
Obdurate mindes : and hearts of Adamant ;
His vertue's fo fublime, that even as foon,
The *Savage Negro's* darts may peirce the Moone,
As the invectives of this froward *Spye,*
A drachme of worth, take from his merit high.

Thus

Thus fpake *Apollo* : while old *Drayton* fmil'd
'To fee him curb'd that had him thus revil'd.

Now when the J*urours* had diftin&ly heard
Each Bill, that was againft thefe men preferr'd,
They then commanded were for to recede,
Vntill they on their Verdi&s had agreed,
Soe pofitive the teftimonies were ;
The evidence s'authentique, and foe cleare,
That they requir'd no man of lawes advice,
For to decide fome points, or matters nice,
After fome time in confultation fpent,
Their verdi&s to the Court they did prefent,
George Withers for their Foreman they had chofe
Who confident was, both in verfe and profe ;
He not did like a Cuftard, quake and quiver,
When he his verdi& came for to deliver :
And firft, of him it was enquired, whether
They in their verdi& had agreed together :
He anfwer'd yes : and then he was commanded
The prifoner to behold : then thy demanded
If that *Britannicus* to them apear'd
Or fit to be condemn'd, or to be clear'd :
The Foreman guilty cryes, then they enquire,
What he can for himfelfe fpeake, or defire,

F 2

Whereby

VVhereby he might evade that fentence juft,
VVhich inftantly proceed againft him muft.
He crav'd his book, but that was him deny'd ;
It was his book (they faid) which him deftroyd.
Nor was this Pris'ner onely guilty found,
For all his conforts heard the felf-fame found.
Apollo then after a conflict high,
Between his juftice, and his clemency,
Not without ebullition of fome teares,
Thus fentence gave upon the Prifoners.
Britanicus condemn'd was to be led,
To that place where the *Porcupines* were fed,
VVhere to a poft faft bound, he muft remaine,
Till with their quils, they had him fhot and flaine.
  But *Aulicus*, *Apollo* did condemne,
  To be tranfported to the *fatall Denne*
VVhich kept thofe *Vipers*, from all parts collected,
Of which *Parnaffus Treacle* was confected.
  For when *Apollo* did long fince defcry,
That Fortune, and the VVorld did much envy
The learned crew, and them to *Limbo* fent,
Oft through the poifon of deep difcontent
Hee through his skill in phyfick did devife
This Antidote againft all maladies ;

                                        And

44

And for this end he did thofe vipers cherrifh,
Among which now, poore *Aulicus* muft perifh :
   But the fly *Scout*, a gentler cenfure found,
(*Apollo* with fuch mildnes did abound)
For he was defin'd to this punifhment ;
He to the *Vale of Hybla* muft be fent,
There to protect the hives of *Thrifty Bees*,
From the Invafions and the Larcenies,
Of *Wafpes* and *Hornets* ; but t'was ordered too
That he ftarke naked, muft this fervice doe,
And he thefe *Robbers* only muft affaile,
With the long feather of a Capons taile,
   The wife *Intelligencer* then did heare
   His fentence, which feem'd fomewhat too fevere :
For he condemn'd was to a *Scullions place*,
Within the Kitchen of *Appollos grace* ;
Where he was forc'd his papers to expend,
Piggs, Pyes, and Geefe, from burning to defend.
   But *Civicus* was fentenc'd to be gone,
Both from *Parnaffus* and from *Helicon*,
And to the Fennes of *Lerna* was confin'd
Where a poore cottage was to him affign'd ;
There he a fory lively-hood muft make,
By angling Froggs out of a ftinking Lake.

          The

The writer alfo of *Diurnalls* was
Condemned to a farre remoter place,
For he was banifh'd to an uncouth land,
Where only *Apes* inhabit and command :
And there he was enjoin'd to inftruct thefe,
In Muficke, and in divers languages ;
Yet had he no more languages then tongues,
No other muficke then the Cuckoos fongs.
But he who did the *Occurrancse* compile,
Was nor confin'd, nor forc'd to chang his foyle,
But by *Apollo's* mercy fentenc'd was,
To ferve with paper all the *Cloaca's*,
That did unto *Parnafsus* appertaine,
And if hereafter any fhould complaine,
He wanted this for neceffary ufe,
Then without bayle and maineprife, or excufe,
He muft be carri'd to that prifon fad,
Bocardo call'd, whence no releafments had.
    The writer of the *True Accounts* then heares
His greviouus cenfure, with unwilling eares :
He was condem'd unto the *Stygian Galley*,
Where he was forc'd upon a wooden talley
To keep a true account of all thofe Ghofts
That daily ferry'd to the further Coafts :

                      And

And for his hire, each night receive hee muſt
Three fillips on the noſe, with a browne cruſt,
Of mouldy bread : and hee for ſeven yeares ſpace
Was judg'd to bee a bond ſlave in that place.
The *Poſt* receiv'd (as it to ſome may ſeeme)
   A ſentence no way rigid, or extreme,
For hee was not exil'd, nor forc'd to change
His calling, for a place of baſenes ſtrange :
Nor was the gallant off-pring of his wit,
Condemned to the Oven, or to the Spitt.
It was decreed he ſhould be ſtill permitted
For to ride poſte, but muſt be ever fitted
With ſtumbling Jades of ſuch decrepite age,
That they would tire, in riding halfe a ſtage.
   Appollo then this judgement did expreſſe,
   'Gainſt th' Author of the *Perfect Paſsages* ;
Hee was confin'd unto a *gloomy Cave* :
Which nor to Sunne, nor Moone admiſſion gave
Here by the glow-wormes blaze, and glimmering
Of rottenwood, he was inioyn'd to write   (light
The Leaguers, Fights, Advances, and Retreates,
Aſſaults, Surpriſalls, and all martiall feates,
Which in that long, and bloody warre were ſhew'd
Wherein ſly *Weaſills, noyſome Ratts* ſubdu'd

                   The˷

The *Spye* then hears his cenfure, which containes
A leffer weight of infamy, then paines.

   For whereas *Phœbus* had receiv'd of late
Petitions meeke, from the *Pigmean State*,
Which fhew'd how the ftern *Cranes* with irefull teen
Oppreft had thefe *Epitomes of men*,
And with their ftratagems, and warlike fleights
Reduc'd that Nation to deplored ftreights :
For they, arm'd with black bills, in combate fierce,
Had foil'd thofe foote and halfe-foote Cavaliers :
And with their watchfull *Camifades* likewife
Did them by night fo frequently furprife,
That they were forc'd to crave *Appollos* aide,
Approching death, and ruine to evade,
Who pitties their eftate, and to comply
With their defires, appoints the cunning *Spye*
To poft away to the *Pigmæan Land* ;
To be affiftant with his helping hand ;
And to difcover with his peircing eyes,
The *Cranes* deepe plotts, and hidden fubtilties :
Apollo likewife did injoine the *Spye*,
To vifit *Caucafus* as he pafs'd by,
Cloud-topping Caucafus, where *Eagles* ftrong
Their airyes have, the horrid Cliffes among :

                            With

With thefe fierce Birdes, him hee commands to
About the levyes of fcme Forces great ;   (treate,
Againft th' infulting *Cranes* to bee imploy'd,
Which the *Pigmæans* poore had fo annoy'd.

   In lieu of other punifhment, the *Spye*
   Was bound to undertake this Embaffye :
And did applaud *Apollos* mercy ftrange,
That did his cenfure to an honour change.

   The *Scottifh Dove* then heard this fentence faire :
Hee to his native countrey muft repaire,
And was on paine of death prohibited,
To croffe the Seas, or to repaffe the the *Twede*,
But while his guilty fellowes did envye
His eafy Mulct, and gentle penaltye ;
Hee cry'd his fentence was fevere, and hard,
And might with moft of theirs, bee well compar'd,
For if they knew the Horne as well as hee,
They'd rather dye, then there imprifon'd bee.

   When judgement was on all the Pris'ners paft,
   Appollo to diffolve the Court did haft ;
But *Aulicus* in moft fubmifsive wife,
For Mitigation of his cenfure cryes :

G

So

So did *Britanicus. Phœbus* relents,
And takes the edge off from their punishments,
They were repriv'd.   Then all the Court commen-
Appollo's mercy : Thus th' *Affizes* ended.   (ded

Printed and Publifhed according to
Order.

F I N I S.

The Spenser Society.

THE Volumes of the Spenser Society now issued constitute the third and fourth which the Council have had the pleasure to send out to the members for the seventeenth year. The previous issues, "The Mirrour of Good Maners," by Alexander Barclay, translated from the Latin of Dominike Mancin, and "Certayne Egloges," gathered by Barclay "out of a Booke named in Latin Miseriæ Curialium, compiled by Eneas Silvius," have given much satisfaction, judging from letters received. Barclay's translation of the "Ship of Fools" was reprinted a few years ago by Paterson of Edinburgh, and it was suggested to him to print with it the works issued this year by the Society. These two works appear in the second edition of the "Ship of Fools." As, however, they did not accompany the recent reprint, and the Council had reason to believe that the reprint was in the hands of many of the members, it was resolved to print the works now under notice. They are of extreme interest, especially the "Egloges," as illustrating the period in which they were written, particularly the Court life of that day.

"The Great Assises Holden in Parnassus," and the "Vaticinium Votivum; or Palæmon's Prophetick Prayer," are included, without question, by Mr. Hazlitt, in his Bibliographical Handbook, amongst the works of George Wither. There is much doubt, however, in the minds of many critics whether George Wither wrote either of them, and in this doubt the President participates. They are, however, of considerable rarity, and are so much identified with the works of Wither, that the Council thought it desirable to reprint them.

The Society is now in its eighteenth year, and looking back on its successful career, the President cannot but painfully feel the loss of the learned and valued friends and colleagues who formed its first Council. Of all that number, and of many that joined afterwards, the Rev. E. W. Buckley alone survives.

A statement has been published respecting the origin of the Society so inaccurate, that the President thinks it necessary very briefly to place on record the way in which the Society arose. In 1867 he was in London, and calling upon his friend F. J. Furnivall, Esq., the Director of the Early English Text Society, he was asked why we did not do something for our early English literature in Manchester. This led to a conversation, in which Mr. Furnivall urged that a Society should be formed in Manchester to reprint some of the rare works of the 16th and 17th centuries. On his return to Manchester, he hastened to the Chetham Library to discuss with its learned curator the scheme suggested by Mr. Furnivall. He found assembled at the Library, Mr. Crossley, the Rev. Mr. Corser, and Mr. Napier, and mentioning the object of his visit, found the project warmly welcomed. Mr. Crossley stated that his friend the Rev. Alexander Dyce, had frequently regretted to him that no complete collection of the works of George Wither, or of John Taylor, had ever been formed, and expressed a strong desire that a complete collection of the works of both writers should be printed if that were possible, but that no publisher would undertake the risk on his own responsibility. Moreover, many of the works would be difficult to procure. Mr. Corser then stated that he believed he had the largest collection of the writings of both Taylor and Wither that had ever been got together, and that they should be at the command of the Society if it could be established. The five gentlemen then present formed themselves into a Committee or Council, and Mr. Corser was urged to allow himself to be nominated the first President. This he declined on account of his advanced age, and Mr. Crossley was then persuaded to take the Presidency. The writer of this notice was named Vice-President. Very little difficulty was found in getting the requisite number of subscribers, and in a few weeks the Society became an accomplished fact.

The publications began with the Proverbs of John Heywood, a copy of which was in the Chetham Library, and it was intended to follow up this volume with the printing of the Interludes, but Mr. Corser's desire that his collections of Taylor and Wither should be pressed forward, from the uncertainty of his own life, caused them to be early taken up.

Mr. John Payne Collier had been reprinting in very limited issue a number of the Early English Poetical Miscellanies, and was desirous to obtain from Mr. Corser the remainder which were in that gentleman's library. One of these, Robinson's "Handeful of Pleasant Delites," was a unique. It is now in the library of the British Museum. Mr. Corser thought that these works would be valuable to the Society, to relieve the monotony of the great series, the publication of which was its special object. These Miscellanies had high poetic merit, and the beauty of the Typography of some of them could scarcely be surpassed.

The Society has now issued upwards of forty volumes, and it may be said for them that as reprints the style in which they have been produced is not equalled by those of any other Society. There are no such collections of the works of Taylor and Wither to be found in any library in the world as those which form the bulk of the Society's reprints.

It was decided at one of the early meetings that no lengthy introductions or memorials should be written, but that the respective authors should be presented to the subscribers with the utmost accuracy, and that the subscriptions should not be wasted in modern matters. The object of the Council was to produce the author himself for study, just as a scholar would go to the original, leaving to future biographers or critics the production of special editions. Perhaps no man was more competent than Mr. Crossley to have written Memorial-Introductions, but he felt that these were quite beside the objects of the Society.

Considering how many works have been lost from our early English literature, and that of many works still in existence very few copies remain, it is of the highest importance to prevent their absolute loss to literature by reprinting such a number of copies as will save them from entire extinction. As already stated, one of the works reprinted by the Spenser Society is a unique copy, and of several of the others very few copies are to be found. If only half a dozen copies of an author's works remain to us, only that number of persons can possess them, and they are in many instances utterly unavailable, not only to general readers but sometimes to literary enquirers. How important is it then that copies should be accessible in every considerable public library.

4

The value of these examples of our ancient literature is not to be estimated from one point of view only. Their poetry may be attractive to one ; the illustrations they give of the manners and customs of the time at which they first appeared may be interesting to another; the modes and tone of thought, the legends, superstition, forms of expression, and even the exemplification of change in language and orthography, may assist the researches of a third. It would be almost impossible fully to realize much that is contained in George Wither's writings without a study of the writings themselves. Even the coarseness and comicality of John Taylor bring forcibly before us a phase of life in the time in which he lived not to be found in the works of any other author, whilst the poem with which the collection of his works opens indicates a power and devotion in the man which some of his other works would lead us little to expect.

The various reprinting and publishing societies, supplemented by the efforts of private individuals, give rich promise that in a few years all our early literature, with the exception, perhaps, of the theological, will be open to every student of English history.

Striking out theology and law, the remaining literature up to the year 1600 might be contained within a room of very moderate dimensions.

Sufficient reasons have been given in former addresses to the subscribers, for reprinting the works of the Society in *fac-simile*.

It is a pleasure to know that very few resignations have taken place since the commencement of the Society. The lapses have been almost entirely by death or by removal to distant places. There are still about a hundred subscribers remaining, and as long as this number can be kept up the Council will endeavour in each year to present works worthy of those that have gone before. The present President cannot expect long to retain the office he holds, but there are members of the Council eminently fitted to carry on the work of the Society when he shall have stepped aside.

JOHN LEIGH,
PRESIDENT.

THE MANOR HOUSE, HALE,
November 25th, 1885.

www.ingramcontent.com/pod-product-compliance
Lightning Source LLC
Chambersburg PA
CBHW030722110426

42739CB00030B/1160